TAKING THE ASHES

God's Response to Sexual Assault

By Crystal Jones

National Human Trafficking Hotline

Hours: 24/7 days a week. Languages: English, Spanish.
888-373-7888
National Sexual Assault Hotline
Available 24 hours
1-800-656-HOPE (4673)

National Domestic Violence Hotline
Hours: 24/7. Languages: English, Spanish and 200+
through an interpretation service
1-800-799-7233

DEDICATIONS

This book is dedicated to all women and children who have experienced sexual trauma. May you find peace, healing, and wholeness in the arms of the King, the One who loves you most.

TABLE OF CONTENTS

1

UNDER THE INFLUENCE

God hates oppression and injustice. His heart about these matters is revealed on the pages of Scripture. Unfortunately, He is mostly ignored. As a result, this world is corrupt and filled with every kind of evil. And its capacity for evil seems to expand by the moment. Every man is doing what is right in his own eyes. Man has taken sin into his bosom and embraced what God has detested.

Our 21st-century American culture has determined that seeking pleasure for ourselves is far better than pleasing God. Our nation is set on seeking every pleasure that is within its grasp, denying itself *nothing*. It doesn't matter if that pleasure is at the expense of someone else. "Do what you determine is best for you" is the mantra of our society.

The media persuades us that we deserve everything that our hearts can imagine. This state of entitlement sends the country spiraling into moral decay, leaving it void of God's holy standard.

Undisciplined and unchecked appetites are dangerous. They lead us right where we are, with no moral absolutes. Indeed, the hearts of men have grown colder and much more wicked.

Unfortunately, many who call themselves believers have come under the influence of this culture. With sin being so pervasive, sadly, men in the Christian community abuse and oppress children and women *almost* as much as men who are outside of it. The stench of sin has wafted into the crevices and under the doors of the church.

The problem exists because we are no longer put off by the things that offend our God. We find God oppressive and irrelevant. The enemy of our souls is at the core of all this perverseness, but he underhandedly charges God with his own crimes. And we concur. "Why did God let this happen? Why does He sit silently by while all this evil happens?" When, in fact, God has not been silent, we've just ignored what He has to say.

Our minds must undergo transformation. We must call right, right, and wrong, wrong. Transformed minds result in changed behavior. That means we must get off the cultural bandwagon and stand flat-footed to advocate for righteousness.

We must intentionally be who God called us to be. It won't happen by following the status quo. It will require that we believe in God, do what God wants done, and say the things that God wants said.

There is a clarion call for true believers to reveal themselves in this hour. And impact the world with love, truth, and justice.

2

TALES FROM THE SCRIPT

A rowdy crowd of men came banging on the door of the old man's house, demanding that he give them the traveler who had just come into town; they wanted to have sex with him. The old man begged this vile mob not to do this horrible thing. But they continued beating on the door, trying to get to the visitor. The old man offered the lustful, rowdy bunch his virgin daughter and the man's wife to do with them as they pleased. How must the two women have felt? It had to shake them to their core. The virgin daughter had to wonder why her father had offered her up to save this man whom he had just met. And the young wife had to be dazed with disbelief. Sadly, this was what their world had come to—vulgar and obscene. The crowd had come for the man. They continued to press against the door in hopes of having the young Levite that had entered their town. The Levite was scared that this old man was not going to be able to fend off this crowd for much longer. In a last-ditch effort to save his own skin, the man cowardly pushed his wife out the door to the violent gang and slammed the door behind her. And the lustful, brutal mob tore at her body and raped her all night long. I imagine the blood pouring from her body as they took turns violently raping her. The brutality and pain forced vomit from her gut as she endured the uninvited torture, and an ocean of tears rushed from her eyes. I imagine she struggled to breathe, gasping and crying, unable to fight them off. Frightened and betrayed, there was no one to rescue her. In fact, the one who was supposed to protect her—the one who convinced her father to let him take her from his house—protected himself and gave her up to such a horrible demise.

When it was morning, she stumbled back and fell at the door of the house with no more breath left in her body. Her husband saw her lying on the ground. He yelled at her to get up. He didn't rush to her side to assist her or try to speak kindly to her. There was no remorse for what he had done. He cold-heartedly and callously yelled for her to get up, but she was dead. The nasty, vile mob had literally raped her to death. When her husband discovered she was dead, he put her on his donkey and took her dead, limp body home. This story is found in the book of Judges, chapter 19.

In another story of sexual abuse, Amnon fell in love with his virgin sister. He was so in lust with her that he felt sick. At the nudging of his friend, he manipulated his father, the king, to beckon his sister to his side. The friend advised Amnon to pretend to be sick so his father would send his sister to prepare food for him. His father complied with his request. Tamar, intent on helping her brother and ignorant of his plans, went about preparing him a meal while he lay in bed. She baked the cakes and emptied them out of the pan for him to eat, but he wouldn't. He urged her to send everyone out of the room. As they all left, he said to her, "Bring the cakes here to my bed and serve them to me yourself." She took the cakes and went over to him. As she offered them to him, he grabbed her and demanded that she come to bed with him. She tried to pull away as she pleaded with him not to do such a horrible and detestable thing. But he would not listen to her. He overpowered her and took her virgin body for himself.

Immediately after he raped her, he was filled with a deep hatred for her; he hated her now even more than he had loved her before. He told her to "Get out!" "No," she answered. "To send me away like this is a greater crime than what you just did!" But Amnon would not listen to her; he called in his personal servant and said, "Get this woman out of my sight! Throw her out and lock the door!" The servant obeyed. Tamar sprinkled ashes on her head, tore her robe, and went away crying with her face buried in her hands. When her brother Absalom saw her, he asked, "Has Amnon molested you? Please, sister, don't let it upset you so much. He is your half-brother, so don't tell anyone about it." So Tamar went to live in Absalom's house, sad and lonely. When King David heard what had happened, he was furious.

Absalom hated Amnon for having raped his sister, Tamar, so he stopped speaking to him. This story is found in 2 Samuel, chapter 13.

God does not hide these stories from our eyes. He lays them out openly in Scripture for all to witness. These heinous crimes were committed by those who were among *His chosen people*. I believe these stories are here for several reasons. One is so we can see that sin is heinous. Rape and murder are not God's will for us. But they are a vicious result of sin on earth. Mankind has a free will with which to navigate life on earth. Unfortunately, that free will is frequently used to go against the will of God.

Secondly, God wants us to know that He does not approve of the base actions of men in the world or in the church. Not only were these actions prohibited by the law, but they were severely punished by God.

Thirdly, God is not afraid of truth. He is the epitome of truth. And though His people can be accused of horrible actions, He is still a righteous and holy God, a just judge.

Finally, I think these stories and others like them are here for us to learn from them. "For whatsoever things were written aforetime were written for our learning, that we through patience and comfort of the scriptures might have hope." (Romans 15:4 KJV)

The truth is, we can't erase history or pretend that these things didn't happen. God doesn't want us to forget. Hopefully, we will look at these things with regret and gain knowledge and wisdom for a better future.

3

WHAT DOES GOD HAVE TO SAY?

G od hates abuse. It is reprehensible in his eyes. Let's revisit the two stories. In the first story of the unnamed woman whose husband offered up his wife to be gang raped, there is a lot to unpack here. The husband, the one who pushed her out into the crowd, had the audacity to want justice. He did not own any of his responsibility for this atrocity. You can read the full story in Judges 19th chapter. He cut his wife's corpse into 12 pieces. And he sent one piece to each of the 12 tribes, saying, "This is what the tribe of Benjamin did to my wife. I want justice."

The way God saw it, that was exactly what they would get—justice through judgment. The 11 tribes of Israel requested that the tribe of Benjamin give up the men who committed this vicious act against this Levite's concubine. But they refused. The elders protected these foul men. So, the 11 tribes of Israel (400,000 men) went up against the tribe of Benjamin (26,700 men) because they would not turn over the perpetrators. God was the One who told Israel to go up and fight. And when they did, Israel lost against Benjamin. You read that correctly: the 11 tribes *lost* against the 1 tribe. In that battle, 22,000 lives were lost. Israel prayed again, and God told them to go up a second time. This time, the 11 tribes lost *again* to the smaller tribe. In this battle, 18,000 men died. So get this: Israel lost 40,000 men in a bloody battle God told them to fight. Forty thousand men died. Why? Because Israel was NOT innocent in this act of violence. It was at a time when everyone was doing what was right in their own eyes. They had forsaken an abiding relationship with God. They were corrupt. The man had pushed his wife out the door. He gave her over to the savages to save his own neck.

Can you imagine a husband who would sacrifice his wife to save himself? How foul! When we know that God is the husband who sacrificed Himself to save His bride. He is the innocent husband who took our place for what we rightly deserved.

In the last campaign, Israel eventually defeated the tribe of Benjamin for the third time. Benjamin was defeated, but there was much bloodshed on both sides. No one really won. *Let it be known that God does not tolerate, condone, or approve of sexual abuse, assault, or whatever you want to call it.* He hates it.

The passage says there was no king in Israel. This heinous act was an indication of the condition of the culture. The deaths of more than 40,000 men in Israel and many of the tribe of Benjamin were because one woman had been sexually abused. This is the judgment God sent to his own people. These were not the heathen nations but God's own people. And if God would judge so harshly for this one woman, He would do the same for all of His daughters.

In Tamar's story, her brother raped her and then disgraced her by tossing her to the side. Had he asked the king to marry her, she could have retained her honor. He was too profane to do so. Her brother Absalom took her in to live with him. Absalom said to her, "Be quiet for now, my sister; he is your brother. Don't take this thing to heart."

Don't take it to heart? She was just raped, and it was by her half-brother—a double transgression. But she was not supposed to take it to heart? Really? How was she supposed to take it?

Absalom hated Amnon for what he had done to his sister; he planned his own vengeance, but he still hushed the victim. He told her not to tell anyone. And when the king heard about the sexual conquest of his son over his daughter, the scriptures say he was furious. Unfortunately, he wasn't angry enough to do anything about it. The king, the ruler with all the power, did absolutely nothing.

As a result, Absalom took matters into his own hands and plotted for two years to kill Amnon. And when he got his opportunity, he succeeded. The royal family was a royal mess.

The men in Tamar's life all failed her. Amnon raped her. Absalom wouldn't let her speak about it. And her father, King David, did absolutely nothing to avenge or comfort the princess. She was left desolate to live with bitter Absalom.

The story goes on for several chapters in 2 Samuel. Each man had a penalty to pay. Amnon paid with his life. And the king had to fight his own son, Absalom, for his kingdom. Absalom humiliated his father by sleeping openly with his concubines. And more than 20,000 men died in the battle between the two men. In the end, Absalom also died.

Sexual sin and abuse do not get a nod from God. Neither does God let it go without retribution. It is sad that the church has not spoken up against sexual abuse more loudly. We have not said that this is NOT the will of God. As a result, some women have been told that it is. Wives are told that it is not rape if the offender is their husband. How absurd! Many have been instructed to remain in abusive relationships and simply take the abuse. Some pastors and leaders have abused their authority and taken sexual advantage of the women in their congregations, leaving God's daughters to sort through the emotional aftermath themselves. It's heart-wrenching.

This book is written to say that God does not approve of sexual abuse in the church or out of it. While the court system may exonerate your offender, and there will be others who may dismiss your claim and refuse to allow you to speak, God is the just judge. He will repay. We have to trust Him with our wounds. His word says, He is close to the brokenhearted. He will rescue those who are crushed in spirit (Psalm 34:18). He will gather your tears in a bottle (Psalm 56:8). And your innocent blood that cries out from the ground must be avenged (Genesis 4:10).

Know this, beautiful daughters: God is for you. He is head over heels in love with you. It is never God's will for a woman, a child, or even a man to be abused. This is the tragic result of sin and of hearts that have no king. This is what happens when everyone is doing what is right in their own eyes. But never is an abuse of any kind the will of God. He is the loving Dad who is for you.

4

UNDER THE COVERS

C hildren and women are being accosted and sold as sexual slaves for depraved men every day and in every state in the U.S. and across the globe. If that is not enough to make your stomach turn, consider this: the average age of a trafficking victim is 12 years old. That means some are older, and yes, some are even younger.

Most of us have a sense of decency and agree that these things shouldn't happen in our society. We are even appalled by them. But are we appalled *enough*? Does it make us cringe when it's someone else's daughter or son? Or do we just shake our heads and keep on doing whatever it is that we are doing?

The number of trafficked people is roughly around 300,000 in the U.S. because sex sells. If so many people are against sexual abuse, pornography, and trafficking, how is it that the sex market is on the increase? It's those who participate in pornography and voyeurism who keep sexual abuse locked in the fabric of our society.

It's the music industry whose singers and rappers promote rape culture and make light of sexual assault. It's Hollywood, with its racy themes and double standards. It's the strip clubs and sexual immorality that aid in keeping a segment of our society chained to sexual abuse and sex trafficking. It's the age-old profession of prostitution (legalized and illegal segments) that keep this rape culture alive and thriving. It's families who won't *out* the perverted family member. All of these arenas covertly and overtly encourage sexual abuse culture.

Pornography is a multibillion-dollar industry. That's a billion with a b. And the market share continues to climb. Any research will prove that there is a strong connection between pornography and sex trafficking.

Even if a person doesn't frequent strip clubs or watch or read porn, he or she can still be found guilty as accomplices in advancing the rape culture and sexual trauma.

We have to pull the cover off our sex-saturated culture with its covert musings, toxic language, and offhand jokes about rape and sexual impropriety. We must stop sexualizing our children. Avoid movies and shows that promote sexual improprieties and try to normalize sexual abuse.

In addition to telling our girls what they should do to protect themselves, the emphasis must be on re-educating our *boys*, teaching them not to rape, harass, and objectify women. We must teach them to respect all girls and women. And we must stop using speech that objectifies or degrades women. We must drive home the fact that "No" really does mean "No!" And not maybe. We must also teach our boys and men to respect the "No" and not try to change it. Our message must be loud and clear: No person has the right to accost the body of another.

A person in America is sexually assaulted every 73 seconds, according to the Rape, Abuse, and Incest National Network. One person in every 73 seconds is sexually assaulted. Read that again. Let it sit with you. It really is quite heartbreaking.

We must be proactive and intentional about addressing this issue. It's not enough to shake our heads and wave our fingers in disapproval when we see that it has happened again to someone in our community.

The worst part of this is that we tend to protect the violators with our silence. When we keep family secrets and hush the violated with "What happens in our house, stays in our house," we are part of the problem. That is the cover-up. These men hurt our families, and because we don't confront them and report them, they are able to continue their assault in the family and outside of it.

Men *and* women cover for the violators, excusing the horrific behavior of the perpetrator, saying things like, "They were drunk," "The women should have had on more clothes," or "They should have carried themselves differently." You can have your opinions about what women should wear or how they should carry themselves, but that still ***does not*** exonerate sexual offenders. The way a woman dresses *is not her consent* by any stretch of the imagination.

If things are going to change, you have to do three things. First, hold the offender liable for his actions. Secondly, look at how you are personally contributing to the issue. What are you watching as entertainment? What is your music of choice? What sexual abuse do you know is happening in your family, school, neighborhood, or community? If you stand vehemently against sexual abuse, I would challenge you to stop victim-blaming or wagging your head. And thirdly, stand up in defense of those who have been molested. Be courageous enough to report all abusers, whether they are your husbands, sons, brothers, uncles, or friends. If the numbers are accurate, then you are probably personally connected to at least one sexual offender. Yes, someone you know is guilty.

Society must change. But society is not some ambiguous "they." You are a part of society. So change must begin with you.

5

ME, TOO

As a first-grader, I was sexually molested by my teenage cousin. Today, more than 50 years later, I still remember this cruel violation. Traumatic memories don't fade quickly. My younger sister and I had to endure the torture of this nearly grown man ravaging our little bodies, barely out of toddlerhood. To add insult to injury, when his brother stumbled upon him in the act, he didn't try to save us. He only threatened my sister and me with exposure. He stood with the perpetrator and accused us as if we were the culprits. Our violator and his enabler led us to believe we had brought this on ourselves. And so we kept his secret.

In today's culture, girls and teens are often dismissed as fast or being grown when they have been stripped of the innocence of their youth by some adult or nearly adult male in their lives. How do you blame a teenage girl for having sex with her teacher, stepfather, counselor, or any adult? Victim-blaming helps the offender. We should be outraged at the men who take advantage of children. These authority figures are not blameless. The children are! These babies have been persuaded, coerced, bribed, and blackmailed. We blame the children as we excuse their offenders.

Rape culture is a culture in which rape is pervasive, prevalent, and normalized through societal attitudes about gender, sex, and sexuality. Sexual violence is normal, and victims are blamed for the crime. There is this normative attitude that says 'boys will be boys' and dismisses personal responsibility. It is quite devastating.

Sexual abuse has been a reality since nearly the beginning of time. We've seen it every time, period. In biblical history, there are various accounts. Over time, white men raped black slaves. Powerful men sexually abused and harassed their employees. Police officers sexually abused citizens. Fathers, uncles, and brothers abused their family members, and no one said a word. The survivor was threatened to keep silent. When it was finally exposed, the survivor was rarely believed.

There has been a shift in the wind. Women have begun to band together and speak out by telling their stories. They essentially said, "It happened to me, too." This strength-in-numbers approach is empowering.

The "Me Too" movement is a worldwide organization formed to fight against sexual violence. Their focus is to create pathways to justice and healing. Women were urged to take back their voice and report those who were violators. The power of me, too, is the "we" factor. It's the strength of many speaking up. As a result, many powerful men have been exposed and lost their positions. Finally, men are being held accountable for their actions.

But before we celebrate too much, we must understand that not everyone agrees with the movement. As women gain the courage to say, "It happened to me, too," there are those who will stand to oppose them or us. They will say it didn't happen or the survivor brought it on herself. She must have wanted it to happen. (Why would anyone want to be abused sexually?) Some will even say, "If it happened, why is she just now speaking about it? Why didn't she speak up before?" They dismiss the trauma that comes with such a gruesome encounter. How sad that someone would take such a position. But they have and will continue.

In my neighborhood, earlier this year, an 80-year-old woman was raped. The perpetrator forced his way into her home, drugged her outside, and raped her while her helpless, disabled husband was inside the home. I didn't know her, but I cried because this happened to her. I cried because I wanted justice. I cried because I am sure she isn't the only senior to whom this has happened. Many in our neighborhood were outraged and banded together to catch the offender. The perpetrator was arrested within the week. The strength of many.

Sexual abuse should never happen to anyone. If we do not speak up, the saga will continue. Our children, our seniors, and our grandchildren will be quoting the phrase as their own reality.

Sadly, my first-grade experience was not my only one. I was fondled, sexually harassed, and molested by others on my way to adulthood. And even as an adult, there was an offender in my workplace that my husband confronted. He had inappropriately touched me and many of my co-workers and pretended it was accidental.

In fear, he profusely apologized when threatened by my husband.

I have three daughters. One was sexually harassed by her boss. One was sexually assaulted by her date. And the other was nearly raped, but her friend jumped in and beat off the would-be assailant. He ran away. Neither of them asked for it or invited it. It happened. Three more "me, toos." You see, the problem isn't with the women; it's with the men, who feel entitled to say and do to women whatever they choose; it's with the men who think it's normal to treat women disrespectfully; it's with the men and women who discount the allegations of those violated.

Will we continue to ignore the broken or discount the voices of victims? Will we continue to support and conceal those who take unwilling participants in their sexual exploits captive?

Fifty years from now, will our grandchildren and great-grandchildren still be saying "me, too" at the same rate? Let the "me too" be in response to "I advocated for a survivor of sexual abuse."

6

UNBELIEVABLE

"They won't believe you," threatens the sex offender to the target of his abuse.

Bill Cosby, R. Kelly, Donald Trump, Harvey Weinstein, and many other famous men have been accused of sexually abusing women and/or children. And when the charges became public, many did not believe their accusers.

Why aren't women believed? I was guilty as someone who didn't want to believe that Bill Cosby, a man with such an impeccable reputation, could do such a horrible thing. But it was hard to deny his culpability after so many women came forward. We sometimes forget that those in the public eye have paid professionals who cast the image or brand that they want the public to see.

One of the reasons we have a hard time believing the stories of abuse from women is because it "feels better" for us to believe the accusation is false. We don't want to believe that our football hero, entertainer, or family is as corrupt as the charges would make him. We want to keep the character or integrity we believe the offender has intact. When we love, respect, or think highly of someone, we have a hard time believing that they are able to do something so heinous. And so we go into denial, holding on to our false realities rather than believing the truth.

An obvious factor is that some girls and women lie and make up false accusations. This is reckless and sabotaging. I personally know of a few cases where the girls and women lied. Most of these fraudulent cases were based on racism. White women accusing black men of sexual assault is common, and it is mostly untrue. In American culture, race trumps gender. A white woman is often believed when the accused is black. In one incident, the woman concocted a false story of sexual abuse to lay claim to extra financial benefits from her job. The innocent man had to pay thousands of dollars to be represented in his court case. He unjustly lost his job, his reputation, and much of his confidence. He was emotionally spent. He eventually pleaded guilty to a much lesser charge with six months' probation. Even though he was innocent, he took the plea because he didn't want to face a white jury as a black man in America. Racism often skews the facts.

In another case, a teenager falsely accused her stepfather of sexual impropriety. She later admitted she lied because she was mad because he punished her. So yes, sometimes stories are made up. But let me say, for the record, the false claims are in the minority. We shouldn't be skeptical or dismiss all cases because a few are untrue.

Some women aren't believed because it would require that we do something. And we are either too afraid or too ignorant, not sure of what to do. It's easier to push this back under the rug.

The final reason that women are not believed is that it is just part of the fabric of our culture to dismiss women and to treat them as second-class citizens. In our society, female pain doesn't matter. Women are sometimes thought to be exaggerating circumstances.

Excusing sexual abuse from men and boys is anti-female and inhumane. I tread lightly here, lest you believe me to be a feminist. I am not. I am pro-men and happily married to a very strong man. However, I choose to side with God. Sexual abuse is **never** okay. And dismissing the harm inflicted on a woman to protect the one doing the harm is unjust.

When our former president bragged about kissing and groping women without their permission and without repercussion, there was not enough outrage. His leaked tape was dismissed as locker-room banter. And he was not held accountable.

Men who sexually assault women think they have a right to sexual access to a woman, even without her consent. Because she is dehumanized or seen as second-rate, they don't see the rape for what it is. It stems from this degrading view of women in our society.

When we discount the stories and disbelieve the children and women who muster the courage to come forward, we set ourselves back as a society. Let's be open to listening to and believing women and children who are making claims of sexual abuse. Let's not dismiss their claims to make things easier for ourselves.

7

SHAME, SHAME, SHAME

Women don't come forward to share their stories because of the shame that is attached to a sexual assault, whether it is in adulthood or childhood. The shame is still there.

The survivor didn't want the abuse to happen. She didn't cause it to happen. She couldn't have stopped it. There was nothing she could have done to sway the predator. So, in reality, the shame does NOT belong to those harmed. Isn't it interesting that the perpetrator doesn't feel ashamed for the criminal act he committed, but the survivor does?

Shame is one of the first emotions that we encounter in Scripture. Adam and Eve disobeyed God, ate the forbidden fruit, and fell into shame as they became aware of their nakedness. As a result, they hid from God.

When we have done something wrong, we can feel ashamed of our actions, and we tend to hide from God, the One who can make everything better.

In Genesis, Adam and Eve were both guilty. In general, guilt is a healthy and useful emotion. Guilt's purpose is to provoke us to remorse. Guilt nudges us from sin into repentance. *Any other reason for guilt is useless and ungodly.* Guilt is only useful when we have sinned. Romans 8:1 reads, "There is therefore now no condemnation to those who are in Christ Jesus, who walk not after the flesh but after the Spirit."

A survivor of sexual abuse is not guilty, nor should she feel ashamed. Neither should the loved ones of the survivor feel ashamed for the actions of the offender. As the authority figure, lover, or advocate for the assaulted one, the family members too often slip into shame, believing that it was their job to keep the survivor safe. And they languish over the assault. Perhaps they were the ones who introduced the offender into the survivor's life. Maybe they feel like they should have done something different or not left the person alone with the assailant. Let me say unequivocally that the fault lies with the offender. The survivor and the family or friends of the survivor are not to blame (except if they participated in the sexual offense). When you feel shame or guilt about someone else's behavior, you are essentially making yourself responsible for their actions. It makes no sense.

The thoughts and intents of others are beyond us. In 1 Corinthians 13:9, it says we know in part. That means that, as humans, we have limited knowledge or insight. Most likely, survivors and their family members acted in good faith and should not punish themselves for the actions of the sexual offender. God certainly does not. Each man is responsible for his own sin.

The survivor is accepted in the beloved (Ephesians 1:6). God calls her his own. He doesn't want her wrapped up in shame. Shame can keep us trapped in our past and make us feel bad about who we are. Shame moves us to hide from God. God wants to disrupt and dismantle the shame we feel. It is Satan's attempt to isolate us, punish us, and push us away from our God, who loves us so much.

Satan attempts to heap heavy loads of guilt, shame, and condemnation on the survivor. This will keep her his prisoner, locked in rejection. He doesn't want her to experience true freedom.

One of the most important things a survivor can do is to reject guilt, shame, and condemnation. His thoughts about you are not condemnations of any kind. He accepts you fully as His child. He does not blame you for what happened. And He doesn't want you to blame you. It will hinder your healing. God is wildly in love with you. He writes your name in the palm of His hand. He thinks about you constantly. The number of His thoughts about you specifically is as the sand on the seashore. He adores you and promises never to leave you or forsake you. He is your advocate. He has an incredible plan for your life, filled with joy, hope, and peace.

To combat thoughts of condemnation, read scriptures on His unfailing love for you. Say them out loud. You are loved (Jeremiah 31:3). You are chosen (Ephesians 1:4). You are God's treasure (Psalm 135:4). You are His jewel (Malachi 3:17).

8

SHH: DON'T TELL

"For nothing is secret that will not be revealed, nor anything hidden that will not be known and come to light." (Luke 8:17)

Although many pastors and church leaders are aware that abuse occurs within their church, there is often little done about it. Survivors are silenced, and offenders go unpunished.

Absalom hushed his sister from the brutal rape of her half-brother. It is important for us to know that if healing is to come, the survivor can't be hushed. If we are going to get to the other side of the trauma, we must open our mouths and speak up about what has happened. We must expose the wound to light in order to get the darkness out. Secrets should be shared, not kept.

Nearly every abuser tells the survivor not to tell. He threatens the one he has exposed and humiliated not to do the same to him. And many comply. Studies show that most abuse goes unreported.

I never reported my abusers. When I became an adult, I told my grandmother about my cousin, who abused me and my sister. She didn't know what to do with the information. It made her uncomfortable. He had already been dead for many years, and I was an adult. She nervously laughed and then told me about her own abuse by a family member. I don't know what I wanted her to do. I guess I wanted her to hug me and say, "I'm sorry that happened to you." But she had never healed from her own secret.

Abuse hurts. Keeping it secret locks the pain in our souls. When we don't allow ourselves to talk about what happened, we tend to question ourselves. "Am I making it a bigger deal than it was?" The survivor hides behind this fallible thinking. She believes the silence will keep her safe, but it only keeps the perpetrator safe.

Keeping the secret also keeps the cycle of abuse in place. The sexual offender is able to continue his abuse under the shroud of silence because he has successfully muzzled his target.

Speaking up is healing and redemptive. Sharing our stories has many benefits. Not only does it out the offender, but it also sounds the alarm for potential victims. It empowers and relieves the survivor. And it helps others speak up.

Certainly, we don't have to tell everyone we meet. But we should say something to someone. Share with a pastor, counselor, or close friend. When we are healed, we can ask God for the opportunity to share our story to help someone else. It may be in a one-on-one session, sharing our testimony, or speaking to a group. It could be a blog, an essay, or a book. The more we speak up, the more we are able to stop the abuse. And help our sisters heal. It's time to turn up the volume on speaking against sexual abuse.

We overcome by the blood of the Lamb and the words of our testimony. (Revelation 12:11)

9

THE AVENGERS

G od takes sexual abuse and assault seriously. He will not close his eyes and turn his head to such atrocities. God loves justice and hates wrongdoing (Isaiah 61:8).

When Jacob's daughter, Dinah, was sexually violated by the son of a neighboring ruler, Shechem, her brothers murdered him, his father, and all of the men of his city in revenge (Genesis 34). In each of the rape cases cited in Scripture, they were precipitated by civil war. In other words, all hell broke loose.

We know God to be our ultimate Avenger. He does not stand idly by with a nonchalant, passive attitude. When a woman is sexually assaulted, God is outraged. In His wrath, He takes action. And it has not been pretty from the accounts we've seen in Scripture.

As believers, we must also be angry enough to do something. We must support and protect those who have been violated. We have a God-given duty to do so.

Biblical law recognizes rape as a violent crime against a woman. The sexual offender was put to death. In Israel, the woman who was raped was believed. She didn't need a witness. As a survivor of assault, she was safe and covered by her community. And the violator would get his just due.

That does not mean we should go about killing sexual offenders. But it does mean we should report sexual abuse, believe those violated, and prosecute those who commit such heinous acts. The Scriptures encourage us to stand up for the oppressed and advocate for justice.

If we let break our hearts the things that break the heart of God, then we cannot keep silent. The severity of sexual assault in God's Law compels *every believer* to listen, protect, and defend the dignity of those assaulted. We must not stand behind the curtain with sealed lips.

God is our Avenger. He advocates on behalf of the woman who has been sexually assaulted. And He expects us to do the same.

Proverbs 31:8-9 says it best, "Speak out on behalf of those who have no voice, and defend all those who have been passed over. ⁹ Open your mouth, judge fairly, and stand up for the rights of the afflicted and the poor."

The Good Shepherd will gather His lambs in His arms and carry them close to His heart (Isaiah 40:11).

10

FORGIVING THE UNFORGIVABLE

So what about forgiveness? How does it fit in the heart of a woman or child who has been sexually violated?

It seems almost unreasonable to even suggest that someone who was violated needs to forgive their perpetrator. It seems like a kindness undeserved to the offender. No matter how challenging forgiveness may be, it is necessary.

Understand that forgiveness is a grace we give to our own hearts. It really has little to do with the offender. Forgiveness helps the survivor feel physically healthy. Many of the physical impacts we feel, like insomnia, heart palpitations, headaches, fatigue, etc., come from unforgiveness. It helps us emotionally, spiritually, and mentally to be in a healthier space by freeing ourselves of the negative emotions that come with bitterness and grudge-holding.

Unforgiveness is a heavy weight. Forgiveness frees us to live our lives without these burdens. Releasing the offense is necessary to get to that healed space in our lives. Forgiveness really is our pathway to freedom.

Despite that truth, I don't believe anyone just gets up from an assault, forgiving. The impact of sexual assault can be lifelong. Often, the survivor has to work through forgiving herself for some things before she can even get to forgiving the abuser.

The human mind sometimes tries to find a way to take responsibility for the harm it absorbs. The survivor tries to retain some type of control by blaming herself. If she had made a different choice, she would not have been in harm's way. Maybe she did make the wrong choice. Maybe she was somewhere she was warned not to go or with someone she should not have been with, but that still does not make her liable for the sexual violation that happened to her. She has to separate the two acts. Forgive herself for the wrong choice. But she still bears no responsibility for the sexual violation.

Healing can't really happen without forgiveness. It is unhealthy to numb yourself or act as if the assault didn't happen. You must deal with it. Forgiveness requires that you acknowledge that something wrong happened.

Forgiveness is a choice. You choose to forgive the offender much sooner than you actually feel it. Your feelings will eventually catch up to your choice.

Forgiveness cannot be coerced by the perpetrator or any of his advocates. Forgiveness is strictly between the violated and God. It is healing for yourself. It moves you from a broken and bitter heart to an open and tender heart, free of the residue of trauma.

I didn't initially forgive my abuser. He was murdered. And I remember feeling relieved that he was no longer alive. Every sight of him was a reminder of what he did. Then, at the same time, I felt guilty for feeling relieved. Guilt, anger, and bitterness had to be processed. I had to work through all of it until I got to where God wanted me: peace and freedom.

Unpacking the emotions that surround sexual abuse can be complicated. You shouldn't try to do it alone. Seek help from someone knowledgeable and compassionate enough to help you work through the abuse. You have to be able to come to the right conclusions. Own what is yours, but lay at the feet of others what is theirs. Then, we can get to true forgiveness.

Forgiveness doesn't mean a lack of accountability. Pressing charges is important to protect other innocent people from sexual offenders. Forgiving does not mean dropping the charges. If the offender loses his job, reputation, etc., that is something he did to himself. Forgiveness also does not mean restoration. If your spouse was sexually abusing your children, forgiving him does not mean giving him access to your babies again. The only time restoration can happen is if the person is genuinely changed. Certainly, God has the power to change men. However, a survivor should not automatically seek restoration. She should reach out to a third party (therapist, counselor, etc.) to help her determine whether real change has occurred and if restoration is appropriate at that time.

Forgiveness is an attitude of the heart. It means you no longer hate the offender or look for vengeance. You don't look to sabotage him or wish him evil. You keep your heart clean and unattached to the offender.

Jesus is able to heal us and deliver us. He has a glorious plan for your life. And He will use your pain to get you to your beautiful purpose.

The enemy does not get the right to define the rest of your life. You have a right to feel free and whole again. Healing comes when you can sort out the fog without being held emotionally hostage by your offender.

11

FINDING JOY AGAIN

"They that sow in tears shall reap in joy. He that goeth forth and weepeth, bearing precious seed, shall doubtless come again with rejoicing, bringing his sheaves with him." (Psalm 126:5-6)

Satan hates all of us. God has made a way of escape for us, but there is none for him. Our path to God is paved with Jesus' blood. When we accept Christ, we are forgiven.

The enemy sets out to either kill our spirit, steal our identity, or completely destroy us and our reputations. We've all been set up to suffer some sort of abuse. His evil plan is to distort the way we see ourselves. He doesn't want us to see ourselves as God sees us. If we don't know who we are in Christ, we won't rise up to defeat him. We will not walk in full victory and access the authority and power we have.

Satan is the originator of abuse. "Beat them, speak death to them, control them, violate them, and hurt them anyway you can. They will blame God and will not run to him. They will be filled with my venom: shame, bitterness, unforgiveness, and self-loathing." He coerces those whom he is able to take captive to do his bidding. Hopefully, you have seen through his schemes and recognize him for who he is.

God's beauties, my prayer is that you will rise up. See yourself as God's chosen, the daughter of the Kind King. He wants you healed, delivered, forgiven, and whole. He wants you to experience His love and grace. Then, you can move on to being healthy and mature enough to fulfill your purpose.

Christ is your rescuer, the One who can save you. He loves you and cares about everything that concerns you. He wants you to have hope of better days ahead. No matter what abuse you have endured, He can redeem it. God can take what the devil meant for evil and extract some goodness out of it. The enemy hates that.

Accepting Christ as your covering, your Lord and Savior, allows transformation to come. God reveals that *you are not what you've been through.* As you submit your pain and trauma to the Lord, He takes your ashes and, in exchange, offers you beauty. He beautifies you as His chosen, His royal daughter.

You are more than a conqueror through Him who loves you so immensely. You are an overcomer. You are not a victim, weak, or subservient. You are stronger than you imagined. You've been through this pain, and yet you survived. You have come out of it changed for the better. The mess of your trauma will be turned into a message of hope. Your testimony will help many others get to the other side of their pain.

It may look dark right now, but know this: The sun will shine again in your life. You will find joy and peace again. You will overcome this temporary setback to settle the score with the enemy of your soul.

So Beauties, Receive God's love. Bask in it. Talk to Him about the hard parts of this journey, and trust Him to navigate you through it. Study His word. Memorize Scripture to help you on tough days. Meditate on His goodness. Even though this terrible thing has happened to you, don't neglect to see the goodness that is all around you.

God calls you healed. Take the steps necessary.

Healed

1. **H**elp yourself. Handle your trauma with the same care you would offer someone else. Get help. Separate from your abuser. Don't dismiss the offense. Speak up. Call the authorities.
   "Make no friendship with a man given to anger, nor go with a wrathful man, lest you learn his ways and entangle yourself in a snare." (Proverbs 22:24-25)

2. **E**xpress yourself. Be open and honest about what has happened to you. You don't have to tell everyone, but you need to tell someone. A counselor, a pastor, a therapist, or a close friend can help you process. You need to talk to someone who can help you unpack your trauma.
   "Keep hold of instruction; do not let go; guard her, for she is your life." (Proverbs 4:13)

3. **A**llow God to love on you. Receive His love and acceptance. Allow God to show you who you really are. Talk to Him like He is your Daddy. Prayer will help you through tough times. God cares about your hurt and wants to help you through it. *"Therefore if any man be in Christ, he is a*

new creature: old things are passed away; behold, all things are become new." (2 Corinthians 5:17)

4. **L**earn to forgive yourself and your offender. You may need to write in a journal or talk to God about it. But release whatever holds you back. Sometimes, you may also need to work through forgiving God. Do the work. God didn't do this to you. Satan is the one who throws the rock and hides his hand. *"Forbearing one another, and forgiving one another, if any man have a quarrel against any: even as Christ forgave you, so also do ye." (Colossians 3:13)*

5. **E**njoy your new life. Open your heart to true joy, peace, and the love of God. Breathe again. God wants you to be free in this life. *"Charge them that are rich in this world, that they be not highminded, nor trust in uncertain riches, but in the living God, who giveth us richly all things to enjoy;" (1 Timothy 6:17).*

6. **D**on't keep your victory hidden. When you are restored, share your testimony of freedom with others. *"And they overcame him by the blood of the Lamb, and by the word of their testimony; and they loved not their lives unto the death." (Revelation 12:11)*

I am not naïve enough to think this will be a short or quick process. It will take time. But keep moving forward. There is light at the end of the tunnel.

12

A Letter to Men

Dear Men,

God created you in His image and likeness. What a great privilege! You are strong, resilient warriors. We are grateful for your presence in our lives. We love you as our husbands, fathers, grandfathers, brothers, uncles, and sons. And we are not afraid to say we need you.

We need your protection, leadership, wisdom, and provision. We need your laughter, your faith, your joy, and your peace. We need you to be the best version of yourself. We are better with you in our lives.

Your image has been distorted by the enemy of your soul. He doesn't want you to know who you are in Christ. He pushes his sexual agenda on you. It cuts both ways. As you harm women, you also harm yourself. You no longer operate in your true identity (Christbearer).

This sexual abuse problem started with you; change can only happen with you. The sad reality is that 90% of sexual abusers are men. So, for those who may have been offended that I wrote this book for women and children, this is the reason.

We need you to step up and speak out on our behalf. We get that many of you have also been sexually violated. Break the stigma and the silence. Be courageous enough to open up and share your own stories of abuse. It was not your fault if you were abused. It doesn't take away from your manhood or identity. You can take back your power from the evil one. Get the help you need to process your trauma. When one of you comes forward with your story, it will make it easier for others, both men and women, to come forward.

We need you to pay attention to your own behavior and speech as well as the acts of others. Own your bad behavior. Admit that you have harmed women or girls. If you have used porn, made cat calls, sexually explicit jokes, or inappropriately touched someone.

Repent before God about the things that you have done and be committed to change. Then apologize to those you've harmed. Accept the consequences of your actions.

"He who covers his sins will not prosper, But whoever confesses and forsakes them will have mercy." *Proverbs 28:13 NKJV*

Get angry enough to do something significant.

Stop watching pornography. If there is no market for it, sex trafficking and abuse will wane. Those who purchase or view pornography strengthen the hands of the trafficker and other abusers.

We need you to enter the ring. Fight with us and for us. Speak up on our behalf. Protect us. Hold your brothers accountable. Don't sit idly and silently while your mothers, daughters, sisters, etc., cry out "me, too."

Change the music you listen to and the movies and programs you watch. Take offense to the sexualizing of our children.

Watch out for your neighbor and the woman standing at the bus stop or walking home alone in the dark.

Intervene when your brothers are yelling at us or physically abusing us publicly. Don't allow your co-workers to get away with offhand remarks. Don't laugh at sexual innuendos. Challenge your brothers to be better.

Most importantly, teach your sons to be decent and wholesome men who respect all women. Be deliberate in instructing them not to rape or be violent with women. Help them understand that they are not to force women to do anything they do not want to do. God gives her free will, and he does not have the right to take it from her. Challenge your sons to cherish women and stand up for us.

Then and only then can we have a better society.

Sincerely,

Your wives, mothers, daughters, nieces, granddaughters, sisters, etc.

www.ingramcontent.com/pod-product-compliance
Lightning Source LLC
LaVergne TN
LVHW051803080426
835511LV00018B/3393